The Ladybird Key Words  based on these common used most often in the E introduced first—with ot appeal to children. All the covered in the early books, and the later titles use further word lists to develop full reading fluency. The total number of different words which will be learned in the complete reading scheme is nearly two thousand. The gradual introduction of these words, frequent repetition and complete 'carry-over' from book to book, will ensure rapid learning.

The full colour illustrations have been designed to create a desirable attitude towards learning— by making every child *eager* to read each title. Thus this attractive reading scheme embraces not only the latest findings in word frequency, but also the natural interests and activities of happy children.

Each book contains a list of the new words introduced.

W MURRAY, the author of the Ladybird Key Words Reading Scheme, is an experienced headmaster, author and lecturer on the teaching of reading. He is co-author, with J McNally, of Key Words to Literacy — *a teacher's book published by The Teacher Publishing Co Ltd.*

THE LADYBIRD KEY WORDS READING SCHEME has 12 graded books in each of its three series—'a', 'b' and 'c'. These 36 graded books are all written on a controlled vocabulary, and take the learner from the earliest stages of reading to reading fluency.

The 'a' series gradually introduces and repeats new words. The parallel 'b' series gives the needed further repetition of these words at each stage, but in a different context and with different illustrations.

The 'c' series is also parallel to the 'a' series, and supplies the necessary link with writing and phonic training.

An illustrated booklet—*Notes for using the Ladybird Key Words Reading Scheme*—can be obtained free from the publishers. This booklet fully explains the Key Words principle. It also includes information on the reading books, work books and apparatus available, and such details as the vocabulary loading and reading ages of all books.

Published by Ladybird Books Ltd Loughborough Leicestershire UK
Ladybird Books Inc Auburn Maine 04210 USA

BOOK 1b
The Ladybird Key Words Reading Scheme

Look at this

by W MURRAY
with illustrations by
J H WINGFIELD

Ladybird Books

Jane and Peter

Jane   and   Peter

Peter and Jane.

I like Peter
and Jane.

I like

Jane likes Peter

and

Peter likes Jane.

Peter and Jane

like the dog.

I like the dog.

---

the   The   dog

Peter likes trees

and

Jane likes trees.

---

trees

A shop.

I like shops.

A a shop shops

Jane is in

a shop

and

Peter is in

a shop.

---

is in

Here is a ball in a shop. Jane likes the ball.

Here   here   ball

Jane has the dog and Jane has the ball.

---

has

The dog has the ball.

The dog likes the ball.

Jane has
a shop.
Here is
Jane's shop.

The shop

has toys.

Jane's shop

is a

toy shop.

---

toy   toys

Here is

a toy dog

in Jane's shop.

Here is

a tree

in Jane's shop.

Peter is in
Jane's shop.
The dog is in
the shop.

Here is Peter

and

here is Jane.

Here is a tree.

Peter and Jane

like the tree.

The dog is here.

Jane likes toys
and
Peter likes toys.

The toy dog
is in the tree.
The ball
is in the tree.

The dog
has a toy.
The dog
likes toys.

I like
the tree.
I like toys.

Here is

Peter's toy

and

here is

Jane's toy.

Jane likes the toy and Peter likes the toy.

Words used in this book

Total number of words 16

The vocabulary of this book is the same as that of the parallel reader 1a.

Now use book 1c.